CREDIT, SCORES and FINANCES

WHAT YOU CAN CONTROL

Table of Contents

By Andres Schonviesner

Quik Know Publishing – www.quikknowpublishing.com

About the Author

Andres Schonviesner has been helping people clear up and build up their credit profiles, and increase their credit scores for 30 years. This work has been done as part of assisting customers to get better home loans when Andres was (and continues) working as a mortgage professional and Real Estate Broker and later when Andres was the owner/manager of a credit reporting reselling company. The reselling company sold credit reports to mortgage companies, car dealerships, and other businesses that had the need for credit reports. One of the services the reseller offered was the diagnosing of credit reports to determine how best, and most quickly, to increase the customer's credit scores. Andres was personally in charge of reviewing each credit report and preparing the diagnosis reports. Andres has helped thousands of individuals to increase their credit scores and get better, cheaper credit because of it.

We will be adding more books and services so check in with us from time to time.

For more information as to services we provide, please visit us at:

www.fix-my-score.com

ONE

What matters and can control

Most people don't know and don't care about, what the difference is between a Fico and a Vantage score is. And they shouldn't. We have no control over which score a lender uses nor will they usually tell us.

What we do care about finding out is how to manipulate the score to our best advantage. How do we make sure that our credit score is as high as possible? This is very important since our scores will affect:

- The interest rate we will be charged
- How much down payment is needed
- Our insurance rates
- Whether we can rent the apartment
- Whether we get the job
- And so much more

In order to manipulate anything, we must first know what it is, what it is comprised of, and how it works.

Let's start with "What is it"

A credit score is just a way of calculating your past experience, with credit, in order to have an educated prognostication as to how you will pay in the future. In other words "do you know how to handle credit and your budget?"

If you watch the TV commercials you would think that we all have 1 credit score. On TV the lady walks into the bank, throws her feet on the desk and announces that she "knows" that she has a wonderful credit score, thanks to the tools on XYZ company's website, and, therefore, demands "what can you do for me" from the loan officer. Is it really that simple? No.

My son recently went onto one of those websites that offer to give you your credit score for free and then went car shopping later that afternoon. On the free website, his score was 698 (very good) at the car lot his credit score was 655 (not so good). How can this be? Both scores were for the same person and on the same date.

I recently helped a friend with their home loan. Her credit scores were 723, 732 and 758, from the three major bureaus. That is a big discrepancy between scores.

How many credit scores do I have?

There are two things that affect how many scores we have, Reporting and Formulas.

The three major credit bureaus, Experian, Transunion and Equifax, each has a basic score for us. But these scores can vary significantly from each other. The scores are based on information sent to them by your creditors. The problem is that not all creditors report to all of the bureaus and they may also not report to each of them on the same date. For example, your credit card reports, to Experian, that your balance is $ 450 on August 1st but reports, to Transunion, that your balance is $ 535 on August 15th and does not report to Equifax at all. Two of the bureaus have correct information about your account, although different, and one bureau has nothing at all. This is a reporting issue and makes your score different for each bureau.

A home loan company, credit card, and a car dealer run your credit report, from the same bureau, at the same time of the same day. Each of these companies gets a completely different credit score for you. Why?

We have different scores because there are different scoring models set up for many different lenders and lending categories. Each model gives a different value to the information that is on your credit report. For example, the credit model that a car dealer would use will give more value to the information about how you paid on your last car loan than what is being reported by your favorite store card, the credit model set up for home loan companies would give more value to your past home loan payment history than to other accounts, etc.

There are probably hundreds of different scoring models, which means that each model may give you a different score on any given day. This is the formula issue.

Scores can vary from a low of 300 to a high of 850. So how is your score(s) calculated? Read Chapter 2

TWO

Scores Calculated

The score calculation is separated into 5 different sections. Each of these sections accounts for a specific percentage of your score.

1) The largest percentage of your score (35%) is based on your payment history. This makes perfect sense since a good way to determine if you will pay future bills on time is to confirm that you have made your past payments on time. Collection accounts, charge-offs, judgments, and bankruptcies are also a part of this section. Negative history will lower your credit score.

Will all late payments, and other negative information, affect your score equally? No. The more recent the negative information is, the harder it will hit your score. A thirty day late on your credit card last month is worth a lot more points, reduced from your score, than a thirty day late that happened 18 months ago. Don't forget that each negative item on your credit will also be calculated differently depending on who is checking your credit report and the scoring model they are using.

2) The next item that affects your score is the percentage of usage (30%). What do I mean? Lenders want to know whether you control your credit or whether your credit controls you. If bank X gives you a credit card with a $ 1,000 limit, will you spend it all or will you spend a small portion? There is a golden rule that applies here:

"**Lenders only give credit to those that do not need it**".

It's obviously not as simple as that, but it is a good rule, although many times unfair. Many people only apply for credit when they need it. If your car broke down and the repairs are going to cost $ 2,000, you may go to the bank and ask for a credit card with a limit of $ 2,000. If that were your only credit card, you have now become a risky borrower. Does it make sense that someone who limits what he borrows should be considered riskier than someone who has 10 credit cards? Possibly not. But the banks are looking for self-control. If I give you a credit card with a $ 5,000 limit can you control yourself to only spend $ 1,000? That is what they are looking at.

Joe has 2 credit cards, with a total limit of $ 5,000, and he owes $ 4,500. Mary has 10 credit cards, with a total limit of $ 20,000, and she owes $ 4,500. Which is a riskier borrower for future lenders? They both owe the same amount. But Mary could have spent a lot more but did not. Joe may be a very conscientious customer, but there is no way for the banks to know this. According to his record, Joe spends as much as he can.

This portion of your credit score does not affect all of your credit. This section is limited to your revolving accounts.

What are revolving accounts?

Open accounts are revolving or installment.

An installment account is one where

1) the amount you borrow is set at the beginning

2) you use the full amount

3) is set for a fixed amount of payments

4) with fixed payments or a written schedule of future payments.

An installment account is closed once you pay it off and you cannot reuse the amount of the principal that you have paid off. Examples of installment loans are car loans, home loans (except lines of credit), personal loans, student loans.

A revolving account is one where you can reuse the credit as you pay the balance down or off. If you pay off a revolving account the account is not closed. Payments are based on what you owed the previous month instead of being a fixed amount. Examples of revolving accounts are credit cards, store credit cards, gas cards.

Why does the usage calculation not affect installment accounts?

Installment accounts, by definition, start off with you using 100% of the loan. When you buy a car for $ 20,000 and put $ 10,000 down, your loan is for the other $ 10,000. Because installment loans are defined by the fact that you will use 100% of it, they are not used to calculate the usage ratios.

The higher your usage percentage of your revolving accounts, the lower your credit score. If you go over your limit, on your revolving accounts, then your score really takes a big hit. This percentage is calculated for each individual revolving account and as a group.

3) The next highest portion of your credit score deals with the age of your accounts. This will be 15 % of

your score. The scoring system will average the age of all of your accounts. The older your history, the better your score.

Sounds simple, right? It is not that simple.

There are several things to consider here.

First of all, the score will consider accounts whether they are closed or not. But if you close the account then it will only remain on your credit report for 10 years, so if you close an old account then you are limiting how old your accounts can be. Also, if you close old credit card accounts then you are reducing your total borrowing limits which will in turn increase the percentage of your limits that you are using (affects the "percentage of use").

Secondly, the system will consider how long the account was in use. If you opened an account 8 years ago and closed it within 6 months of opening it, that account is a 6-month account and not 8 years' worth of credit history.

Which is better? Joe opens a credit card account 7 years ago then closes it a year later OR Mary opens a credit card account 2 years ago and is still using it? Joe will be scored as having 12 months' worth of credit history while Mary will be scored as having 24 months. Mary will have a higher score. What could have Joe done differently? Joe could have left that account opened and used it once a year to pay for lunch. Joe would now have 84 months of credit history and a higher credit score.

My oldest credit card is 29 years old and still ticking. The limit is too low to really be of any major use, but it pays for lunch twice a year and then I pay it off the following month. The average age of my accounts is 6 years and two months. Does my 29-year-old card help my score? You bet it does. Without my oldest card the average age of my credit would drop to 3 years. I pay $ 12 a year to maintain this card and it is well worth it.

4) Account mix is also a part of your credit score. It will be 10% of the score. Account mix means that the scoring system is looking to see what type of credit you have. Do you have only credit cards (revolving) or do you have a home loan (installment), car loan (installment), 2 credit cards (revolving) and a gas card (revolving)? The more diversity in types of credit, the higher your credit score can go.

But what if you don't own a home and your car is paid off? What can you do to have diversity?

One option is to consolidate your credit cards with a personal loan. The personal loan will be an installment loan with fixed payments for a fixed period of time. But remember, that unlike a credit card, a personal loan cannot be reused once paid off so do not pay it off early when possible. **You are trying to get diversity but also a long time of use**. Get a three-year term on the personal loan and pay it as agreed. Even if the amount of the personal loan is small (ex: $ 1,000 personal loan), the idea is to get a mixture of types of accounts not the size of the account. Let me clarify one thing, the personal loan must be from a bank, credit union, or an entity that reports to the bureaus. A personal loan from Uncle John will not help. Also, try and stay away from loans given by last resort type of lenders. A payday loan is an installment account but does not look good on your credit report.

5) The final part of your score comes from inquiries. Inquiries will make up for 10% of your score.

An inquiry occurs when someone checks your credit report. There are two types of inquiries, soft and hard.

A soft inquiry occurs when an employer checks your credit for employment purposes, an insurance company checks your credit for insurance purposes, an existing lender checks to see if you qualify for an increase in your credit limit, etc. So a soft inquiry is not for the purpose of issuing you a new credit account in the future. A soft inquiry will not be shown to other creditors and do not affect your credit score. Only you will be able to see it on your credit profile.

A hard inquiry means that you have applied for a new credit account. These inquiries are viewable by anyone checking your credit report and do affect your credit score. Inquiries will remain on your credit profile for 2 years.

Why would a hard inquiry affect your score? Remember the golden rule we spoke about before;

"**Lenders only give credit to those that do not need it**".

Well, the golden rule applies here also. Every time you apply for credit your score is lowered. One inquiry may drop your score by 2-3 points. Ten inquiries, within a short period of time, may drop your score by 100 points. Why? The more inquiries you have, the more a lender will think you need credit.

1) Too many inquiries and they will believe that you are desperate for credit,

2) If you are desperate then there is a financial hardship,

3) if there is a financial hardship then you are a risky borrower,

4) **Lenders do not like risk**.

As always, time is your friend. Inquiries will disappear in 2 years. If you need to open a credit account then apply to two or three on the same day if possible, then wait for 6 to 12 months before applying for anymore.

There are a few exceptions to this rule. If you are shopping for a big ticket item such as a home loan or car loan then all inquiries that pertain to this shopping, that are done within two weeks of each other, will be counted as one inquiry. The problem happens when the lender does not classify their inquiry correctly. For example, you go to your local bank shopping for a home loan and the agent runs your report using their "credit card" subscriber number. Companies that do more than one type of loan usually have different accounts from which to run your credit report for each type of loan. Existing customers being checked for increases in credit limits (soft inquiries) will have their credit checked using one system while someone applying for a car loan will be run using a different system. As long as your lender uses the correct system you should be fine. Ask your lender if their system is being used for only your purpose.

Based on this information we can see that those with excellent payment history, that is aged, with many different types of credit, low balances compared to their limits and no inquiries will have the highest scores.

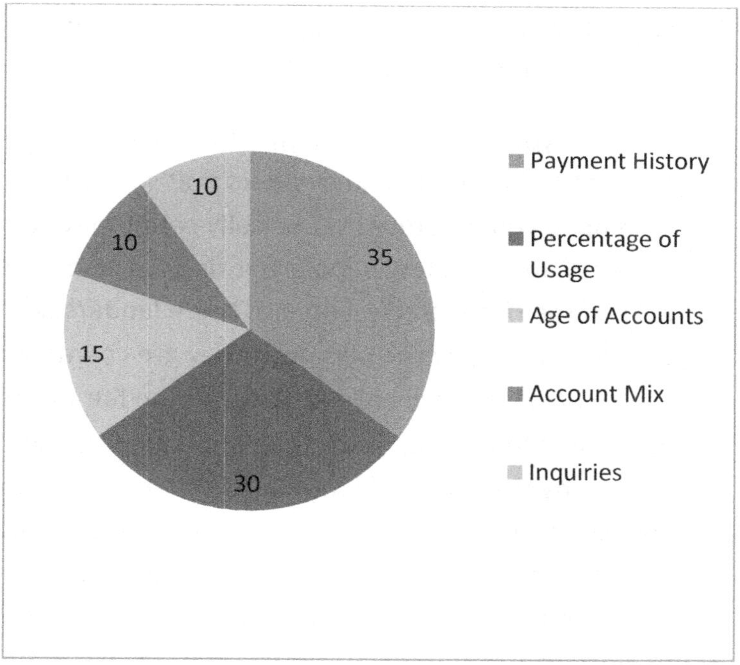

THREE

How do I start my credit?

Getting credit for the first time, or building up limited credit, may seem hard to do. Most lenders will not want to take the risk.

If you are a college student it is a little easier to get credit. There are many lenders that specialize in lending to college students. Actually credit may come **too** easy and with few people warning you about the risks of too much credit. Some of these lenders don't care if you can pay the bills now, they are counting on the fact that you will have income later in life and they are willing to wait for you to get your career going. Of course, by then they will have put your account into collection thereby ruining your credit and increasing their fees tremendously. If you get credit, while in school, make sure that you do not borrow more than you can pay. Your credit will determine if you get the job, get the apartment, and get the car loan. **Your credit profile is the most valuable thing you own**; don't destroy it because you just could not do without that bigger TV or trip to Vegas. Think long term and your life will be better for it.

If you are not a student and are looking to start or increase your credit profile, there are things you can do. First of all, you will need to have income in order to get credit. I know this sounds like it should go without saying, but you would be surprised how many people don't consider this.

One way of establishing credit is to get a secured credit card or loan. This type of account requires that you open a savings account, with the lender, and deposit the same amount of money you wish them to lend you. This savings account will be restricted; you cannot take out the money, and it will be used to guarantee payment on the loan or credit card. The lender is basically lending you your own money and charging you a fee for dealing with the accounting and reporting to the credit bureaus. Since the lender is not risking any money, they will be more willing to give you credit. Not all banks offer this service and you may want to check with credit unions in your area or look for some online. Make sure you confirm with the lender that they do report to **all three** credit bureaus. You want to work with lenders that report to all three so that you are building your credit profile with all of them. If they only report to one or two bureaus then don't open that account and look for another lender. After 6 months of making payments on time, ask them if they would convert your account to an unsecured account. If they do then you can close the savings account and use that money to open another secured account with a different lender.

Another way of starting credit is to apply for store credit cards with the lower priced stores. Most of these stores will take a chance on you for a small amount of money, usually starting you off with $ 200 to $ 500 in credit. Stores such as Target™, Walmart™, furniture stores, and stores that market to the Spanish community are good places to start. This may mean that you are purchasing something that you really don't need but building credit will cost you some money. Just don't buy anything too expensive. When I was first establishing my credit I went and purchased a slightly overpriced watch ($200) at one of these stores on an installment loan basis. I paid $ 20 a month for the next two years. It helped me get started and it will help you also.

You want to get a total of 2 to 4 credit cards and one installment loan if you can afford it. Just make sure that you can make the payments. Having a bad credit history is **worse** than not having credit at all. Also remember to use a small portion of the credit card limit, and then pay it off, a couple times a year. For the first year, have a balance owing every month, on the secured credit cards. The lender will not switch the account, to unsecured, until you have a history of making your payments on time.

No balance due = no payment due = no payment history with the lender

No balance may look great on your credit report, but your lender knows the whole story.

Can't find any secured credit cards? Go to

www.fix-my-score.com

FOUR

I have bad credit. Now, what?

If you have bad credit there are several steps you can take to make sure you turn it around as quickly as possible.

Step One – Make sure your information is accurate.

The first step to cleaning credit is to make sure that your credit profile is accurate. We start off by requesting a free credit report, from each bureau, by going to www.annualcreditreport.com. These reports are free, by federal law, and will not be counted as an inquiry on your profile. Since you will get a separate report from each of the three bureaus, you will know who is reporting what and to whom. Very important. Now review each report for accuracy and duplication. Is your name spelled correctly? Are all of your addresses correct? Are there any duplications? Many times your lender will sell your loan to a collection company and now the debt will show up twice or more times. We will talk about how to correct your information later in this chapter.

Step Two – Pay off negative accounts

The collection, past due, charge-offs, tax liens and so forth are negative accounts and need to be paid off if you want to re-establish your good credit. But not all accounts should be paid.

Take a look at when the lender has last reported the account to the bureau. The normal collection, past due, and charge-off accounts will only remain on your credit profile for 7 years. Bankruptcies, tax liens, and other public records will remain for 10 years. If your lender has reported your account as a charge-off but has not updated the information in the past few years then there is a chance that they will not ever update it and ignoring the account may be the best thing to do. Let sleeping dogs lie. Remember that time is your friend and that the older the negative comments are, the less value they have on your score.

If your lender is reporting the negative information regularly or currently then you will need to deal with it. The best option is to talk to the lender and see if they would be willing to remove the account from your credit report in exchange for payment. This is optional to them, they are not required to do so. But it cannot hurt to ask, especially if it is a collection company. You may also want to ask for a discount in exchange for a full payment. It is rare when a collection company will be willing to give you both the discount and the removal from your credit, but those that do not ask will never receive, so ask away. Also, make sure that whatever agreement you negotiate is given to you, in writing, prior to you making any payment. Once you have the agreement in writing, make sure you follow thru with your part of the bargain. If you know that you will not have the money until 15 days from now then negotiate that your payment will be made 30 days after the agreement is reached. Everything is negotiable at this point.

If your lender sold the account to a collection company, and both are reporting the account, make sure that the original lender shows that the account was transferred and has the correct date of the transfer. This will get rid of the duplication of bad credit.

If the negative information is already paid off or is a public record, such as a bankruptcy or tax lien which is paid off, make sure that the final status of the account is correct in status and date on your profile. If you have a bankruptcy, does it state that it was discharged? Is the discharge date correct? Do the accounts that were discharged by the bankruptcy show the filing date of the bankruptcy as their final date? Do these accounts show a zero balance? If you had a tax lien, does it show that it was released (paid off)? Is the date of release correct? If the paid off account is a collection or charge-off, is the paid off date correct?

Once you have cleared up your bad credit as much as possible then you should go back to chapter 3 on how to start your credit profile, the steps are the same in order to re-establish your credit. But do the clean-up first. You would not cook a dessert, in the same pot that you cooked a stew, without cleaning it out thoroughly first. It's the same thing here.

To clear up information on your credit profile, send a DISPUTE letter to the bureaus needing corrections. Most of the bureaus have a dispute entry page on their website but if you can't find it or would rather do it in writing, their addresses are in Chapter 10.

I would highly suggest that all disputes be done online directly with the bureaus. Written requests will need you to include your social security number and date of birth. If these letters were to get lost in the mail, who knows what may happen to this information. Dispute requests may also be done thru your account with www.annualcreditreport.com.

Can't find the right credit cards, go to

www.fix-my-score.com

FIVE

Should I use a Credit Repair company?

There are a few things you should consider before hiring a credit repair company.

1) Can they do anything that you cannot do yourself?

2) What are they actually promising to do for you?

3) What kind of guarantee will they give you?

4) If they don't do what they say they will, how do you get your money back?

Let us take each of these questions one at a time.

<u>1-Can they do anything that you cannot do yourself?</u>

The quick answer is NO, they cannot do anything that you could not do yourself. The laws are very clear and the bureaus are not going to get into trouble just to mess with your credit report. They don't know you and don't care if your credit is good or bad, they just care that it is as accurate as possible. If you file a dispute with the bureaus they will send it off to the reporting lender and ask for confirmation of accuracy. If the lender responds that you are correct or does not respond within 30 days, then the information is removed or corrected. If the lender responds that their initial information is accurate then the information stays as it is and your next choice is to contact that lender and get the information corrected. If the lender will not do so then you may have a legal case against them and you should consult with an attorney. If the negative information is accurate, and yours, then it will probably remain on your credit report. Don't fall for promises to remove all bad information, they are rarely true.

Now it may be that you could do it but you don't have the time, patience, or desire to do it yourself and would rather use a company to help you. That is okay too, but read the rest of this chapter first.

<u>2-What are they actually promising to do for you?</u>

In most cases, the credit repair company's contract will state that they have earned their fee as long as they have changed information on **<u>ONE</u>** of your accounts. Forget about what the salesperson tells you and read the contract before you sign up. You may find out that the verbal promises and the written contract are very different. When the verbal promises and written contract are in disagreement always trust the written contract.

If they only promise to change information on one of your accounts then you may want to use them AFTER you have done everything you could on your own.

3-What kind of guarantee will they give you?

A money back guarantee is only as good as the company giving it to you. Who are they? What is their track record? Can you verify any of this without just taking their word for it? Be skeptical.

4-If they don't do what they say they will, how do you get your money back?

Will you have to sue them to get your money back? Are they local or out of the area? Are they a corporation and are they registered in your state? Even if their contract makes it seem easy to get your money back just remember that it is only a piece of paper. You may wind up having to go to court. If the salesperson is local to you, are they willing to guarantee the work themselves? In writing?

Unfortunately the people that need help the most are usually the easiest ones to rip off. Do your homework before paying any money upfront or signing any contract for future payments.

I have provided you with some sample dispute letters, which I have used in the past, at the end of the book.

SIX

Increase your score 60 points in 30 days

First of all, the title of this chapter is possibly an oversell to some while very achievable for others. Whether you can do this or not depends on the status of your credit at this time. If you have bad credit it will probably take more than 30 days to fix. If you have excellent credit then you may already have the highest score possible for you. So let's make sure you know how to maximize (manipulate) your credit score no matter where it is today.

The first thing we will need to know is what your score is today. You will not get a score from www.annualcreditreport.com. In order to get a score, you will have to pay for it, from each bureau, or you can get them for free from some of the free credit websites such as;

www.creditkarma.com™

www.creditsesame.com™ or others.

These are important since they will update your score monthly and keep tabs of how they have changed.

Once we have your score you will want to look over your credit report to make sure it is accurate (see chapter 5).

Finally, we will do two things that are easy to do for long term gains and that take a short time to accomplish. It may require you to spend money.

The first thing to do is to look at your revolving accounts (credit cards, gas cards, store cards, etc). In order to have the best score possible, these accounts should have a balance due that is no more than 30% of their limit. This means that if card "A" has a limit of $ 1,000 you should not owe more than $ 300 on that card. If you have the cash to pay these down then do so, if you do not have the cash then maybe you can pay the debt down on credit card "A" by using credit card "B". But follow the same rule for card "B".

Example:

Card "A" has a limit of $ 1,000 and balance of $ 550

Card "B" has a limit of $ 1,000 and balance of $ 100

We need to bring down the balance of "A" to $ 300, so we need $ 250. Card "B" can be increased to $ 300 and we only owe $100 so we can use $ 200 of it to pay down card "A". Now both cards are at 30% of their limit. You can accomplish this by paying card "A" online with card "B", by asking card "B" to pay down card "A", or with a courtesy check from card "B". Please note that these transfers usually have fees charged. Consider these fees in your calculations.

Make sure that you have at least 3 revolving accounts that have a small balance owed. Why is it important to owe money? Your score is a snapshot of your credit. Imagine if you were in school, were an excellent student, knew the subject forward and backwards, but never turned in any homework. What kind of grade would you get? If all of your revolving accounts are paid off the credit scoring system cannot tell whether they have been paid off for years or whether you paid it off last month. A big part of your score is how timely you pay your debts. This means you have to have debt. If all your bills are paid off, go charge up the cards a little and do not pay them off. Now if you don't care about your score and want to increase it when you need it, then you can have everything paid off until you want to increase the score. Just remember that it will take 30 to 60 days for your lender to report your new balance to the credit bureaus, so plan accordingly.

The second thing we will do is take care of any negative items on your credit report. Follow the instructions in Chapter 4.

If you find this too complicated or would like a professional assessment, please go to our website, **www.fix-my-score.com**, and sign up for our personal consultations.

SEVEN

Setting up a budget

The best way to keep your credit in good shape is to live within your budget. So setting up a budget is very important.

A budget does not need to be difficult or complicated, you can use a notepad, a spreadsheet program (my favorite) or an accounting software.

There should be two major parts of your budget, the income, and the expenses.

<u>Income</u> – The income portion should be set up just like your paycheck is set up. It should show your gross income and all of the different deductions from your paycheck. The reason we do this is so that we can easily see where our money is going before we get it.

Example posting –

Gross monthly income –	1,850.00
less Federal tax withholding	- 175.50
less State tax withholding	-112.75
less Social Security tax	-115.62
less 401K deduction	- 80.00
less medical insurance deduction	- 145.00
Net monthly income -	1,221.13

It is important to know where your income is going before it gets to your pocket because not all of the items are mandatory and even those that are, can sometimes be adjusted. In the prior example, if we needed more money for bills we could cancel our 401K deduction (it would give us an extra $ 80 a month to pay our bills). Another possibility would be to reduce the amount is taken out for federal and state taxes (but consult your tax professional first).

Expenses- On the expense portion I include several sections:

1) Large expenses – such as rent, car payment, utilities, food, gas, insurance, car registration (prorated)

2) other required monthly expenses – such as credit cards

3) nonessential expenses – We may each have a different distinction for what is nonessential but at the beginning all expenses that do not fit into one of the other two areas should be placed here.

Example posting –

Rent	$ 850
Car payment	275
Electric bill	95
Food	350
Car Insurance	180

Visa card # 1	25
Visa card # 2	30
Starbucks	120
Bowling	75
Movies	70

The amounts on some of the expense categories may change monthly, for example, how much you spend at Starbucks™ will not be the same month to month, same with the gas, food, and other expenses. **It is important to keep a record of these types of expenses on a daily basis**. You can keep the receipts and record them later or do as my daughter does and write the expense into a journal when you pay for the expense. You will be surprised how much you spend on a daily basis.

Once you compare your net monthly income to your monthly expenses you can determine whether everything is okay or whether you need to make a change. If you need a change, it may be to increase your take-home pay, reduce your expenses or a combination of the two.

Increasing your take-home income comes down to either increasing your income by working more hours, getting a better paying job, etc. or by reducing the deductions taken out of your paycheck. Look at voluntary deductions such as 401K plans, voluntary savings accounts, etc. Do you need them at this time? A 401K plan is a great thing to have as long as you can afford to eat and have a place to live. But if it is a choice between putting gas in the car and putting money away for retirement, I would put gas in the car. I can always start saving later for retirement. Another thing to look at is to find out what your tax returns will look like at the end of the year. For example, if you are a single person and your total income for the year will be $8,000 then the question is whether you will have any "taxable income" for the year. If you will not have any "taxable income" then there is no reason to have any money withheld, from your paycheck, for federal or state taxes. You can use that money now. How do you find out what your "taxable income" will be for the entire year? You can ask a tax professional or use last year's tax forms with this year's numbers (it won't be exact but pretty close).

Reducing your expenses will also be easier once you can see exactly where your money is going. Start by looking at the big expenses and thinking about whether they can be reduced. You should be shopping for car insurance every two years. Your driving record and experience is changing all the time. You may be able to get cheaper rates from a different insurance company. Look to see if there are any deals available for your telephone, cable, Wi-Fi services in your area. Could you switch to store brand food instead of national brands?

Maybe buy gasoline from a cheaper brand? Could you reduce the interest rate on your credit cards? I rarely pay more than 3% interest rate on my credit cards; I'll explain how you can do this in Chapter 9. Can you get a roommate?

On the nonessential expenses, try and get more specific as to their classification and which ones you can live without (or at least with less of). Are they truly nonessentials to you? Can you live with going to Starbucks™ once a week instead of every day? Could you rent movies from Redbox™ instead of going to the movies every weekend?

It is said that a problem cannot be fixed until it is identified. Putting your expenses down on paper will help you live better. Setting up a budget for the future requires knowing if you have any money left over after paying all the mandatory bills. Write down how much you think you should spend, as a maximum, on nonessential expenses. Complete a separate list for each month and compare your progress each month. Most of us don't make huge changes quickly, the reminder of what you are doing and where you want to be will help get you there.

Example of a budget

Income

Gross monthly income	2350.00

	Federal tax deduction	-245.00
	State deduction	-108.00
	Soc. Security deduction	-146.88
	401K deduction	-100.00
Net Income		**1750.12**
Expenses		
	Rent	850.00
	Electricity	55.00
	Gas (for home)	42.50
	Water bill	30.00
	Cable TV/WIFI	105.00
	Car payment	145.00
	Car Insurance	98.50
	Groceries	275.00
		(target is $ 250)
	Gas for car	100.00
		(target is $ 75)
	Credit card A	25.00
	Balance is $ 2250 at 21.99%	
	Credit card B	50.00
	Balance is $ 1397 at 15.99%	
	<u>Entertainment/nonessentials</u>	
	Coffee shop	85.00
		(target is $ 35)
	Movies	115.00
		(target is $ 50)
	Eating out	175.00
		(target is $ 75)

Total Expenses

2131.00

Net Income (1750.12 – 2131.00)

-380.88

Based on this example, I need to reduce my expenses quickly and reaching my target budget will not be enough. I may need to increase my take-home income.

EIGHT

Setting up a balance sheet

A balance sheet is used to see where you are financially and what you are worth. The balance sheet is comprised of two sections; 1) the assets and 2) the liabilities.

I set up a separate balance sheet per month and update all of the balances on the same day of each month. This allows me to see whether I am progressing or regressing when it comes to how much I am worth.

1) The Assets – An asset is something that has value. Personally I only count those things that I can sell for cash if needed. Examples are; your car, bank account, collectibles, stocks, the cash value of an insurance policy, etc.

My Assets section may look like this;

Assets	
Checking account	1,800.00
Car value	10,500.00
Savings account	395.00
Total Assets	12,695.00

2) The liabilities – A Liability is a debt that you owe. Examples are; the loan against your car, credit card debt, etc. On my liabilities portion of my balance sheet, I include the following;

1) name of lender
2) last 4 digits of card number
3) interest rate
4) date interest rate changes
5) balance owed
6) minimum monthly payment

1) name of lender – If you have more than one account with the same lender then this could be Bank of X Visa™ or Bank of X MasterCard™.

2) last 4 digits of card number – for identification use only

3) Interest rate – I want to know which cards have the highest interest rate so that I know to pay these off first.

4) date interest rate changes – Many new credit cards come with an introductory interest rate for the first X number of months. I want to know when this rate will change.

5) balance owed – Balance as of that date. I usually call the automated service of my lender to get an exact amount.

My Liabilities section may look like this;

Liabilities

Bank Y car	1122	10.50% until 12/5/2019	(8,622.05)
Bank X Visa	2211	12.99% until 5/1/2016 - 22%	(1,201.00)
Bank Z Visa	3344	18.99% forever	(2,000.00)
Total liabilities			(11,823.05)

Total Assets and Liabilities (assets minus liabilities)= + 871.95

This shows me what I am worth today, $ 871.95. But what else does it tell me? This document tells me who I should pay off first if I can afford it. Which bills you pay off first should depend on several facts.

The first thing to consider is whether you will need that money back if an emergency occurs. For example, you have an extra $ 100 a month in your budget and you would like to spend it to pay off your debt sooner rather than later. Great idea! But what will happen if your car needs repairs next month? Will you wish that you had not spent that money on paying down that bill? Do you have money saved up for such an emergency? If you have reasonably good credit, I would suggest you think of your credit card as your savings account. If you pay down the credit card (not store or gas cards) then you can use it to pay for the emergency while saving on the interest rate when there is no emergency. If your credit is bad then I would not take the risk that the lender will not close your credit card account. I would set up a savings account for emergencies before I pay any debt down (more than the minimum payment due).

Secondly, if you have plenty of excess money or are comfortable using your credit card as your emergency funds, then I would pay off the highest interest rates first. Benjamin Franklin is famous for having said "**a penny saved is a penny earned**". Saving money is actually more valuable than earning more money. Money earned is taxed, so a dollar earned may not be worth a dollar while a dollar saved is always worth the full dollar. If you are just starting out your credit profile please remember our rules in Chapter 3.

One of the ways that we keep our credit profile in good shape is to prepare for the unforeseen. Have either a savings account or available credit for the emergencies. Life happens to all of us, be ready.

NINE

Pay less than 3% interest on credit cards

For the past 7 years, or so, I have been paying 3% interest, or less, on my credit cards. This does not include store or gas cards, just the MasterCard™ and Visa™ cards. What I do, does require good, but not perfect, credit and reasonable income (based on your limits).

Step One – Have more credit available than you need.

Besides having my credit cards at 30%, of their limit, I also keep credit cards that are completely paid off. Lenders want to give credit to those that don't need it, but they don't make money unless you use their credit cards (which is where step Two comes in).

Step Two – Use the No interest cards.

The lenders whom I do not owe would like me to owe them money. These lenders mail me special offers to consolidate my other cards with them at No interest plus a transfer fee, or a very low rate, for 12 to 18 months. The transfer fees vary from 2 to 5 percent upfront. When I get these offers I use them to pay off the credit cards who are charging me higher rates.

Step Three – Use the newly paid off cards

Once the low-rate period ends, on the credit cards I used to refinance my debt, I use offers from the cards I paid off previously to refinance the new debt. This way I never pay the normal 13 to 25% rates that the credit card companies charge.

Step Four – I did not get any offers for a lower rate

If I do not get any offers to consolidate my credit cards at a low rate then I ask for them. I start by calling my existing credit cards and asking if they have any deals currently being offered. On one occasion, the lender told me that their offer was included in my monthly statement for the last 4 months. I had never seen it because I did not have a balance with them.

If my existing lenders do not have any offers then I apply for new cards that do offer a lower rate.

Recently my son was shopping for a used car. Although he has good credit, the lender was offering him a 13% interest rate. We used low-interest credit cards to buy the car and he is now paying 2.99% a year in interest. Plus, since the car is not financed, he can get a lower priced insurance policy for the car.

Ten

Sample Dispute letters

The letters attached are letters that I have used in the past. They are not meant to be used as legal advice. If you need legal advice then please see a licensed attorney. I would use the bureau's websites instead. Both the addresses and websites are here.

Send your dispute letters to the bureaus at the following addresses:

Experian Consumer Assistance Center
P.O. box 4500
Allen , TX 75013

Att: dispute dept.

Or **www.experian.com/consumer/upload**

Trans Union
P.O. box 2000
Chester, PA 19022

Att: Consumer dispute Center

Or **https://dispute.transunion.com**

Equifax
P.O. box 740256
Atlanta, Ga 30374

Att: dispute dept.

Or **www.ai.equifax.com/creditinvestigation**

Date: enter date

To: credit bureau
Their address

Re: **<u>Complaint letter to delete inaccurate information</u>**

To Whom It May Concern:

I formally request that the following inaccurate items be immediately investigated. They must be removed in order to show my true credit history, as these items should not be on my report. By the provisions of 15 USC section 168li of the Fair Credit Reporting Act of 1970, I demand that these items be reverified and deleted from my record.

Item No. Company Name Account number Comments

 # 1
 # 2 **use one letter per person per bureau**

Since 30 days from the receipt of this letter is your allotted time under the law to reverify these entries, it should be understood that failure to do so within that 30 day period constitutes reason to promptly delete the information from my file
(FCRA 15 USC s 168li (5) (A)).

Also, pursuant to 15 USC s 168li (6) (A) of the Fair Credit Reporting Act, please notify me when the items have been deleted. You may send an updated copy of my credit report to the below address. According to the provisions of 15 USC section 168lj, there should be no charge for this notification. Also, please send me names and addresses of individuals you contacted so I may follow up.

Sincerely,

Sign your name

Include your address, date of birth and social security number
If you have moved within the last two years include your previous address

Date: enter date

To: credit bureau
Their address

Re: **Request for removal of outdated information**

To Whom It May Concern:

Please note that under Section 605 and 607 of the Federal Fair Credit Reporting Act you are obligated within 30 days to delete obsolete information from my consumer credit report. The following items on my credit report are more than seven years old and exceed the statutory time period under this Act, and they must be removed:

Item No.	Company Name	Account number
# 1		
# 2	**use one letter per person per bureau**	

Also, pursuant to Section 168 of the same Act, I am entitled to notification that the items have been deleted. Please send an updated copy of my credit report to the below address, as well as to any other party that has inquired about my credit rating in the last six months.

I anticipate your immediate attention to this matter.

Sincerely,

Sign your name

Include your address, date of birth and social security number

If you have moved within the last two years include your previous address

enter date

To: credit bureau
Their address

Re: **Reminder to respond**

To Whom It May Concern:

Thirty days ago you received my letter disputing several items listed in my credit report, issued by your firm. The items were inaccurate and incomplete. I have attached the original letter.

Under the Fair Credit Reporting Act 15 USC 168li (5)(A), you had 30 days from receipt of this letter to respond to my request for reverification of the erroneous items. I have not received a reply from you within these 30 days. Therefore, it must be that the information on my report was either inaccurate or could not be reverified. In either case, according to the provisions of 15 USC section 168li (a), the items must be deleted immediately.

Please respond immediately so that I do not need to pursue my legal rights under 15 USC section 168ln or 168lo, which require compliance with the law.

Also, pursuant to 15 USC section 168li (d) of the Fair Credit Reporting Act, please send me notification that the items have been deleted. Send an updated copy of my credit report to the address below, as well as to any other party that has inquired about my credit rating in the last six months. According to the provisions of 15 USC section 168lj, there should be no charge for notification of changes on my credit report.

Sincerely,

Sign your name

Include your address, date of birth and social security number
If you have moved within the last two years include your previous address

enter date

To: credit bureau
Their address

Re: **Request to merge inquiries with account**

To Whom It May Concern:

The presence of inquiries as entries separate from accounts on my credit report inaccurately duplicates information. These inquiries reflect an incomplete and inaccurate processing of information in my file. The inquiry entries should be removed, or at least merged into the accounts to which they belong. The accounts in question are:

Company Name
Account Number

-
-
-
-

Enter information here

-
-
-
-

Under the provisions of the Fair Credit Reporting Act 15 USC section 168li, please reinvestigate and delete these disputed items. Send me names and addresses of persons contacted. Thirty days from receipt of this letter is the length of time you are allowed under 15 USC s 168li (5)(a) to complete these actions unless you immediately notify me otherwise. It should be understood that failure to reverify within this time constitutes non-verification, and the items must be promptly deleted according to Section 168li(a).

Also, pursuant to 15 USC section 168li(d) of the Fair Credit Reporting Act, please notify me when the items have been deleted. Send an updated copy of my credit report to the below address. According to 15 USC section 168lj, there is no charge for notification of changes on my credit report.

Sincerely,

Sign your name

Include your address, date of birth and social security number
If you have moved within the last two years include your previous address

enter date

To: credit bureau
Their address

Re: **addition of consumer statement**

To Whom It May Concern:

I have disputed the accuracy and completeness of incorrect information on my credit report. Since reinvestigation has not resolved my dispute, I want the following statement, without alterations, included in my credit report to set forth the nature of my dispute for others to see:

Write your explanation here

According to the Fair Credit Reporting Act 15 USC section 1611i(b), I have the right to enter this "consumer statement" in my credit report. The Act also states that you are obligated to include my statement in any subsequent consumer report that includes the disputed information. Furthermore, because my statement contains less than 100 words, I demand that you include the full text of the statement in my report, without changes, alterations or summaries.

Pursuant to the Fair Credit Reporting Act, please send me a free updated copy of my credit report with the above statement included. I assume that 15 days from your receipt of this request represents a reasonable time for completing this update, unless you immediately notify me otherwise.

Sincerely,

Sign your name

Include your address, date of birth and social security number
If you have moved within the last two years include your previous address

enter date

To: Your creditor
Their address

Re: **Explanation for delinquent Payment on account number "enter account #"**

To Whom It May Concern:

It has recently come to my attention that several of my payments to your account have been labeled "late" on my credit report.

These missed payments were due to:

Explain each late here, be detailed and worthy of sympathy

I have been prompt in paying in the past, and since the late payments occurred for the above excusable reason, please correct the payment history for my account at the following credit bureaus, which carry your account histories:

Enter name of the bureaus needing correction

It is important that my credit report reflect the good relations I have had with your company in the past. The corrections in the credit report will make it more representative of my financial habits.

I appreciate your assistance.

Sincerely,

Made in the USA
Monee, IL
04 November 2026

67352874R00036